From an Upstairs Window

Poems by
Brady Peterson

ISBN: 978-1-945917-13-4

Printed in the United States of America

Front Cover Image: Melinda Peterson
Author Photo: Barbara Peterson

The following poems were previously published:

"Level", "Measuring Gaps", and "Still Open
    to the Public" — *The San Antonio Express*
"A Bakery Revisted" — *The Enigmatist*
"Still, the Urge" — *all reads will lead you home*
"They Report the Lakes are Full "— *Blue Hole*
"Carbon" and "A Focal Point"— *Red River Review*
"A Summer Night"—*Ilya's Honey*
"Love Letter #2371"—*Nerve Cowboy*

Also by Brady Peterson:

Glued to the Earth
Between Stations
Dust

BIG TABLE Publishing

"Making other books jealous since 2007"

Big Table Publishing Company
Boston, MA
www.bigtablepublishing.com

*For Mark
who breathes poetry*

Table of Contents

They Report the Lakes are Full

From an upstairs window—pear blossoms white,
each perfect. Tiny green figs peek out from winter,
milder this year, though tornado warnings
Monday remind us mild and nature
are hardly comfortable dance partners.
A red tail perches on a highway pole,
scanning the grass for mice, a delicacy.

Four miniature porcelain fat Buddhas
huddle on a window sill, a gift from a student,
expressing a certain rebellion against Baptist
orthodoxy. On the desk, a cross with an engraved
dove holding an olive branch in its beak,
another gift—sent when my daughter
died.

This is how we touch—how we remember.

It rains for four days, but now a pause.
Puddles of water on green grass. We had meant
to plant tomatoes Sunday. And basil—
dancing the space between a possible late
freeze and an early summer when it grows too hot
for the tomatoes to set.

The Delicacy of Wood

How do I explain the joy
of working a rip saw—
feeding it long one by twelve cedar boards
and binding, with metal straps,
the swirls of one by twos spit out
from its teeth.

Three things a lumberman
hates, old Tom tells me in confidence,
wet—dry—and that God damned one by two.
I marvel how a board goes into the saw
so straight and comes out gnarly,
like spaghetti to be stacked and strapped
straight again.

My grandfather lost a thumb
to a rip saw when he was a young man.
My father, who hardly showed much
concern, openly worried about my working
the yard. Watch yourself, he tells me.

I unload shingles and shakes
from boxcars—riding a three wheeled
fork lift inside— lean back a little
to keep balance. I slide redwood
from bins, flip cedar from
the top of open stacks,

lose my hold once and fall
so quickly to the ground I miss
the measure of it. Unhurt but
startled, I lie silent on crusher fines
between stacks of lumber.

I am twenty-five with a fresh degree
in English and an honorable discharge.
I am twenty-five with a one year
old daughter I call Pooh.
I am twenty-five, the world
still in front of me.

A Bakery Revisited

Give a bum a twenty dollar bill,
or seven cents of your terrific money—
eighty years. Must take inflation into account.
Good night, you say—*boa noite*. He grins,
a white bandage on black skin.

Try the milk rolls—or gooey tarts.
Who else would describe parked cars having tin
hides—the moon gazes on the street.
Mean habits—the banality of slack trolley wires
stretching into the chocolate of night.

Eighty-one years before he was born,
an assassin jumps from a balcony. *Sic semper*—
Booth or Brutus—or Virginia…
Some still alive when he was born who remember,
though through a gauze.

Not bread alone—yet the smell of baking
loaves from the nearby bakery in the morning
when loading cedar beams onto the fork lift,
using leverage and forearms—yeast rising—
offering a sense of well being.

Meeting by Chance

It would be interesting to discover
you sitting across the room at a table in a coffee
shop, waiting for me to look up.

Where have you been, I ask. How long—
your being there renders the question moot.
I look up from my notebook.

This thing we call the mind—carbon variations
of digital code, nothing explains my seeing
you in an imagined circumstance.

Could lead to a kiss or lovemaking,
but conversation is equally appealing.
We dance a tango to a silent music.

How deeply I have loved, the poet explains
to a crow sitting on a leafless branch.
He walks the alley to the plaza.

Dots on the Horizon

A spell against falling objects—the smell of cooking
grease—with a gritty determined mind, with pen
and notebook, he plucks madness from order,
or order from madness—no matter.
From breakfast 'til noon on lined paper.

Listens to a couple talk at a nearby table. Trouble
with the data, the woman complains to a companion—
I can't squeeze it in. She is pretty, he thinks, or might
have been if the corners of her mouth—but pretty
is a gawking term.

The mind, or the heart—an avocado,
sliced and served with the fried eggs and hash browns.
Something must count. Ink and paper, a ship
off the Gaza coast, the deep blue Mediterranean Sea.
My God, someone screams.

December 1955

Eisenhower's Washington—winter, snow falling.
My brother and I pose on the steps of the capitol—
the first coats we have worn in three years—
the first snow we have seen.

A snapshot in black and white. Back in the car,
the need to push on—always. We drive US 1 southbound.

I secure a quarter for the television set in a motel room—
I am nine, and English TV is novelty.
My brother and I share half a back seat, the Buick
packed tight. A hamburger bought at a drive in.

I am sick and throw up on the side of the road.
Years before I could eat a hamburger whole again.

We turn west and drive for two days toward Christmas—
our grandmother greets us with tears, the bakery
smell of her house. A left-handed baseball glove
under the tree.

Beginning Its Fall

Around the curve of the earth—can you see—
straight line limitations, the trajectory arc comes
faster than sound. A crowd gathers—a mob,
depending on linear equations.

You stand on the second highest ground in the county,
look east where the land starts to smooth its way
toward the gulf, the soil turning to black gumbo—geese
fly north overhead. You hear them honking
to one another in some ancient tongue. The round
planet, the round sun—a vapor trail.

The honking geese are magical—flying crooked
wedge lines. They veer toward the lake,
then turn away. You watch as if watching a lover,
hanging onto a last glimpse. She climbs into a car
and never looks back.

Firewood

I spend an afternoon splitting firewood, the muscles
in my back and arms, shoulders—the synchrony
of both letting the blade fall and driving it hard.
October yellows and reds, the air crisp, the smells
of an opening chapter.

Lars smokes his pipe—flannel shirt grins.
Do you feel it yet, he asks.
He is thirty. I am twenty-four.

Lars is the strongest man I know—chiseled, handsome
to a fault, absorbs work like a sponge.
That evening we sweat in a public sauna,
then plunge into a cold pool.

He calls me years later, the week my mother dies.
Do you feel it now—yes.
We need to get shit faced drunk again sometime, you and I.

Aquavit kept in a freezer—
after chopping wood, after sweating naked—
the opening lines of a book one meant to write.

Using Wadded Bread as Bait

A boy and girl play together inside
a billboard next to a highway, the billboard
a spaceship—You and I imagine ourselves
travelers to some distant planet where apples
and oranges and two bright suns. What fun
we had—though Monday at school I didn't
talk to you.

You huddled with your friends, I with mine.
At lunch I beg a nickel from a classmate
to buy a fudge bar in the cafeteria. We play
flag football on a hard sand playground—
I run a gauntlet of boys grabbing
for a piece of cloth. You are talking
quietly with another girl.

Here on Earth, with its solitary sun,
with highways that carry one past billboards
and cities. One morning, after the last day
of school, we climb in our packed car and leave.
That summer, in another State, my brother
and I fish a pond every day, as if the pond
would somehow make up the difference.

Sincerity

There is Mozart the genius and Mozart's the coffee house
on Lake Austin where we met once or twice
and talked about how love endures, or not. I misplaced
the thread connecting us, it seems. No matter—
the narrative carries all possible, don't you see.

I sometimes go a week now, he confesses,
as if he dropped a stitch—sometimes even forget.
He frowns, then forces a smile,
the muscles in his face—a passing photographer.

We pose—we pose. The nose powdered
and turned slightly toward a setting sun.

Gathering

Ezra's fascination with Mussolini dispels
the notion that a poet—I can't explain, a friend
says while we tend the smoker, feed splits
of oak to the fire. I have oatmeal on the stove,
but coffee is enough for now.

What were the choices—all bad, I think.
One sinks like a descending balloon
leaking helium. We cook beans
in a pressure cooker. Slice cabbage
for slaw.

I saw the sunrise this morning having
salted and peppered the brisket when it was still
dark. We eat and read our poems on the patio
and imagine a world with bluebonnets
and bees—Mussolini, Stalin, Hitler dead
and dusty.

Still, the Urge

If I am not home here, then where—
Did you hear the sound this morning.
Yes, you say—some bird, not a hawk—
we walk the river, map the currents,
and talk about taking a canoe downstream
toward the gulf. If not now, when—

but not now. The hassle of loading,
the necessity of leaving a second vehicle
at some crossing clutters the simplicity.
Still, the urge tugs at your sleeve—
You remember a time when you almost
drowned in this water—

though upstream twenty miles,
before the dam, before the lake.
We are too damn old, you grumble.
Still, the urge.

A Summer Night

We lie to children, unable to bear
the emptiness of what we know—
My daughter realizes heaven is full
of dead people—just a bunch of dead
people, she says. She is four.

Death is a door, we say when fireflies
glow in the evening. A summer night
in Arkansas—the air thick with the smell
of bark and honeysuckles. The knob
turns, a door opens, then shuts.

Someone you loved—love still.

Fried catfish with French fried potatoes,
sweetened ice tea—the ice clinking
in the tumblers. They drove past our house
on the way to the restaurant, my cousin
says. I waved at them.

We sing old songs, the ones we sang
as children when the only radio was AM
and fuzzy. We walk the street of a town
where we lived, waiting for my father
to come home from the war.

The church on the corner where
my brother asleep slipped from his
front row seat to the floor—the preacher
steps from behind the pulpit, reaches
down and picks him up without

skipping a beat in his sermon.

Passage

When the road from Fulton was gravel,
we sat in the back seat watching our father
take the hill crossing the railroad tracks,
up and down—the sudden drop leaves my
stomach behind. A favorite part of the ride—

almost out of body—We pass the cemetery
on the left in Saratoga where my brother always
loses his cows. Every time. My father is buried
there now. My mother—her parents. Everyone
we thought important.

When I was ten, my grandfather sent me out
to hunt in the pasture alone with a twelve
gauge single shot Savage. I kill a bird
on that hunt, the weight of the gun—
the kick.

Sleeps Through the Morning Alarm

A friend loses sleep at night
worrying—big hearted tender—oppressive
summer nights when one can hear
music playing from the cantina next
to the river downtown—*wisdom blues,*
he tells me—true wisdom weighing the heart
which is more than muscle, pumps more
than blood.

Cicadas sing the dark—Imagines
a man and a woman meeting on a street corner,
getting into a cab—a thin sweat of June
on her skin—a street lamp—she and the man
settle in for the ride. There is no context—

Imagines sitting on a front porch counting
fireflies—listens to the old people talk
about a great uncle long dead who came home
changed—wouldn't hunt anymore. Drank
himself to death, they said. His wife left him
for a salesmen in Nashville.

Dreams he is in a room with strangers—
trying to explain entropy. A man in a white
jacket offers him a drink. People clump
in small groups talking in b flat.

Place

You take a breath, watch the sun rising
on a December morning. Here leaves are starting
to fall. Here it's more the subtlety of colors.
Missing are the dramatic reds and purples
you saw the October you spent
in Maine—after mustering out of the navy,
a wife and new baby in tow.

You help wheel a barrel of cider
to the back door of a house left unlocked.
If someone wants in, they will simply break in,
perhaps splitting the door—out here in the country
where no one will hear the noise, your host tells you.
It's his brother's summer house, and he is storing
the cider in the cellar to give it the time necessary.

That afternoon, his wife gives you a copy
of Kafka. You are reading Solzhenitsyn
for the first time, almost everything for the first time.
Bellow, Heller, Fowles, Greene—eating books
as if you were starved. Taking a short trip
from Maryland to Maine to visit an aunt,
before heading back to Texas.

Turning

March will be difficult, if it comes at all—
always the caveat now. Henbits crowd the raised
beds. He digs the roots with a hand trowel—
shirtless in mid February. Just yesterday,
the wind howled. Just yesterday, they bundled
themselves in layers of wool.

The cold burrowing into the bone—an eagle
flies from a limb twice in three days—a nest
nearby perhaps. We had not seen eagles
before this past year. We walk
the path near the river. Water is being
released from the dam upstream.

Only a few hundred yards from the new
subdivision—newly paved roads, foundation
forms being nailed into place. Fourteen
new homes ready now. The wild being
squeezed into narrow ribbons
along river bottoms. New homes
waiting for children and toys.

Measuring Gaps

He feels the time appointed—
anointed, oil and lavender, the stench
of rotted meat—O, Israel—or was it Bozeman,
Montana on a summer ride. Red-winged
blackbirds in a field. Look—

I've seen them before, the boy says.
Of course, he's only eleven. You are twenty-nine,
thinking if one could learn to adjust the valves
on a '70 VW bug—compression lost
and the car wheezes to a halt.

The engine cold and the car on flat
ground. The manual takes you through the steps—
pages smeared black with handling. Knuckles
scraped. Step by step, utility mingling with beauty
found in a common place.

You learned to bake bread, tune your car,
plant your first tomato plant. Read Plato
in the stacks of the old graduate library.
John Barth—does anyone read him now—
sot-weed, any plant growing wild.

Still Open to the Public

We make love in a park on a Saturday morning,
hidden in the bushes but still broad daylight,
seemingly out of sync with your being so private
a person, but not if one thinks it through.
We listen to cars passing close by.

The capacity for the simple joy of running
in a summer heat then soaking your head
under an outdoor faucet. I count the ways and days
of walking the evenings to the capitol
when it was still open all night to the public.

We sit in the stadium seats on a Wednesday
to watch the band rehearse. A reporter
and photographer stop and ask us why.
Free entertainment, we answer. We are
wrapped in it—the notion of what is dear.

I Shall Pick the Flowers Myself

September, and I am already pushing spring
in my mind, though winter is pleasant enough—
no mosquitos. Late August showers, spindly rain
lilies—don't remember seeing them before—
showing themselves for a few days.

I saw you working your garden, bent over a row
of beans—driving by last week, last month
it may have been—wishing I could paint
the impression, but am more than a hundred
years too late.

Too late to celebrate the feelings one once had,
Virginia says, before the light of shell fire
revealed the world—puffed and stuffed
with straw—still I saw you working your garden,
wanted to paint you there—

Mixing colors on a palette, white cotton trousers—
as in wearing them cuffed—greens and browns
wildflowers on the side of the road, lazy susans
and daisies—brushed yellows. Summer gives
way to September—then October.

Pumpkins and cranberries, whipped cream
and whiskey in your coffee, a twinge of regret—

Counting

The battery runs low on my drill,
and the backup won't take a charge—
a screw left half way in—a break
in the water line up the street—
crews are working on it.

I stink from the morning run, from working
on the deck before the drill went dead—
no running water for a shower
nor even a cup of coffee. I dig an old hand
drill from the bag, the kind you crank,

set a star shape bit in its teeth, then lean
precariously over the railing to finish
driving the screw through the old wood—
I earn my keep this way—with myself,
with the ghost of my father, with Calvin

and his Puritans—a good name for a rock
band, I think. I sip mineral water from a bottle,
count my toes—more and more
distant. Tomorrow, power wash
the deck, then paint it—several coats of thick

paint formulated to fill cracks. A man
on the phone invites me to read my poems
to his literary group next month. Two questions
for my introduction, he says. Do you have any children—
do you have any pets. Five and no, I tell him.

If You Feel Like Clapping Your Hands

We cannot find your records, Gil—
did we look for them. Late at night,
driving from Austin on PBS—did I hear

it right, my daughter's expression asks me.
She grins the way someone grins when suddenly
smacked by the bright light truth of a thing—

something a friend recently said was unknowable,
yet can you feel it in the bone if you are open enough,
ready enough—if you occasionally run barefoot.

We stop to fill up with gas. Candy and chips
under neon. Paying with plastic—money
not being real. Nor miscellaneous jazz.

A Footnote

Notes found in a family photograph album
say he was born in New York Harbor, his parents
coming from Ireland, fleeing the great famine,
his finding his way into the Confederate Army
at fourteen, a flag bearer—captured then released

at the end of the war. He becomes a riverboat captain,
meets Addie in New Orleans—marries her. Lives
happily, we suppose, though he dies at thirty-six
from tuberculosis picked up in prison camp.
They have a single son, my great grandfather.

Addie remarries then dies suddenly one day. Her husband
buries her quickly, as was custom, though some claim
her body was still warm—a story my mother told,
having heard it when she was a girl,
when women sat in wooden chairs shelling beans.

Love Letter #2471

I dreamed you and I last night captured Hitler
and turned him over to Eisenhower.
Otherwise the dream was pretty weird,
and you were blond not brunette. I was thirty,
as always. Your husband was in the scene,
but didn't have a speaking part. Ike
took Hitler off our hands. The war
continued.

I should be wearing a cool hat
if you're going to put me in a dream,
you say. Who decides these things.
Hitler and Ike both looked like newsreel
copies. Both movie stars
from the pre-McCarthy days.

I'm usually in a grocery store in mine,
you tell me. Looking for Lorca in the produce
section.

Jams

Sun tanned and pretty after a week
on the Galveston coast,
getting stuck once in the sand.
Some guy in a truck appears
as if part of the script and pulls
your car free.

Sleeping the night with tiny crabs—
cold water public showers,
eating oysters raw from the shell,
beer bought with an altered ID—
spur of the moment road trip in August
after quitting your job hauling bricks

and dancing the night with a Eurasian
girl who told you her father
would skin you if he knew—
even what you were thinking.
She grinned and you slipped out
the back with Brian.

The Present Site

A dig into ruins sometime distant,
though maybe not so far—a hundred years,
a thousand. The dust of brick and mortar—
dried apricots sealed in foil. What people
were these—assumes someone or something.

We talk briefly after your reading. I walk to my car.

You were very good, I say. You smile.

Not even dust in the gears.

Or maybe more than dust.

How does one explain the desire we have to touch
the mind, however impossible, to feel not so alone.

The idiocy of walls. The Manchurians.

The smell of oranges.

He remembers the men still young drinking rum
at the officers club. They had survived the war
with Germany and then North Korea—
still in their twenties. He listens to the tones
of their voices. Yearns to be among them,
though he was only eight going on nine.

He kisses a girl on the cheek outside the service club
after play practice.

A grass stained baseball rolls into the yard. He picks it up
and tosses it back.

From a window in a downtown building, he watches
a circus parade. He plays the slots with the nickels
the bartender gives him.

Level

When the truth of a thing no longer counts
in the equation—from a penthouse window
four miles off, he watches with naked eye
jumpers leaping to escape the burning fuel—
thousands upon thousands cheering in the streets—
I saw them, he claims. Others come forward,
saying they too—the mind corrupts easily.

When power becomes beautiful, when winning
is all that matters—when theater becomes real—
the line between a rapist and a bricklayer
working with mortar on a Thanksgiving morning
is blurred— I walk past the men working.
We exchange nods as they gently tap
each brick into place.

March Madness

My neighbor is yelling
at his riding mower. It's rained
for a week or more, and the grass
has bolted like a Haitian rebellion.

My neighbor on his back, his hand
reaching under the mower as if to untangle
some cord. I can't hear what
he is yelling, only that he is.

Trick or Treat

You carve an imagined pumpkin with a carving tool,
not a simple knife, but something sharper and curved,
so that one gives expression to Jack's face—
a sneer so subtle you only notice it after walking away.
A warm breath on the back of your neck.

You turn. It grins at you—Jack's candle glows, glimmering
through its eyes, its mouth. You hold still as if waiting
for a word to be whispered. You hold still in the space
between—you listen to the walls, the floor,
the ceiling, the windows, the door—you listen.

Jack grins. It's not all it's cracked up to be.
This being alive or dead, real or not.
The coming and going of the children—the old. You feel
the cold in your bones, the ache of it—deep.
You reach for chocolate.

Portrait

After school, after eighth grade basketball practice,
a classmate shows me a photograph—a naked
woman, an image in black and white,
the first I'd seen of its type. *Look*—revealing
some guarded secret. The classmate grins, and I wonder
how I am supposed to react.

I feel there's protocol but don't yet understand
the rules. This being a boy. I am wearing a jacket.
It's cold but not freezing. The woman was not pretty,
I don't think. But pretty is in the knowing—
I look at the photograph for a few seconds,
hours.

I dig through memories stored in the garage
with the half used paint cans—
The woman whose face I can't remember
must be dead now, or very old.
I find myself wanting to tell her I'm sorry—
for staring but not seeing.

Port Hueneme

A man wades into the surf, fully clothed—
to his knees, his waist—waves crash
into his chest. He holds his arms out above
the swelling ocean. Two police officers
watch him from shore. One talking
on her phone.

I think about Virginia
and the heavy rocks she drops
in her pockets—about the corpse
my children saw washing up on the beach
some years ago down the coast.
Pelicans fly by in a line.

The man is running from the cops,
not trying to drown himself.
The second officer stands at the edge
of the surf calling to the man, but too distant
for me to hear. Wave after wave,
the man bobbing.

The man finally relents. Officers guide
him to a waiting squad car. He grumbles
about the injustice of being—of the ocean—
They wouldn't let me see her—my own
wife's funeral, he moans.
My own wife's funeral.

She wasn't his wife, a man behind
me says. Just a girlfriend. He killed her,
with his drugs and booze— or might
as well have— as if someone needed to explain..
The man's face pressed against the window glass.
I walk the beach the morning after a wedding.

Spine

He escapes into a sliver of wild,
the trail marked with bread crumbs
and empty beer cans—always light beer,
it seems—so wild is more a figure of speech.

Still a stream runs here, and coyotes
yap at night—wild turkeys gobble—
An old stillhouse built in the tight canyon,
next to the stream, over a bubbling spring—

He peers inside. The floor planks rotted.
A tribute to the old Volstead Act days
when resourceful proved determined.
He turns back to the path,

the stream falling toward
the river below.

Routine

A helicopter gun ship flies
low over the house—
returning to a nearby base.

I feel the percussion
of blades beating the air—
feel it in my ribs.

I move about the kitchen,
loading dishes to be washed—
the walls vibrate in empathetic synchronization.

I am part of the movie though insignificant
to the plot, an extra—spear shaker,
I miss the lunch buffet,

wedges of melon and tuna fish sandwiches.
Have signed away any claim
to my image.

More than once,
walking the fields alone,
I look up and wonder.

Chant

Soffit is a builder's word, a carpenter's word—
like fascia and header and stud. Top plate
and joist. Soffit though has a mantra quality.
Whisper it over and over as you slip into deep
meditation. *soffit, soffit, soffit…*

As if to quietly call the angels to your side,
whispering low so they have to move in close
to hear. What is it you want, they ask—*nothing.*
What is it you want—*nothing.*
Want being deceiver's word, a labyrinth.

The soffit seals the attic, keeping out squirrels
and raccoons, though a determined creature
may find its way in. You set out a trap.
Raccoon may be a mantra word as well,
though you hesitate to use it.

It's raining. You check for leaks,
an old habit. You listen to the rain
as if the patterns were code one deciphers,
rain being a sacred gift—like air.
What is it you want—*nothing.*

You are dry and warm inside your house.
Puddles form on the driveway.

what we keep

sorting the piles of what was once
too precious to throw away,
but hasn't been used—or even gazed
upon for twenty or thirty years,

stored in plastic cartons and stacked
in the room behind the garage,
spilling out into the garage—the trunks
your mother had the help carry

up the flimsy pulled down ladder
to the attic, now covered with cobwebs
and dust, filled with love letters
written in high school—hers or yours.

she saved everything, even napkins
from a birthday party when you turned six.

Here I Am

I dream you older and fleshy last night,
at a banquet eating—the room crowded
with people I should know—it's my dream
for Christ sake, but all strangers to me.
The speaker waiting to speak.

You look up and see me, then return
to your plate. I wake to a cold room.
I close my eyes, but the dream is gone.
The sound of rain on the roof—
my roof...   but nothing is mine—

It's all just here— a painting called real,
but just a painting. Your hair grayer,
your cheeks fuller, your arms—
I want to impress you somehow,
some gesture.

Circumstance

He remembers when the milk man delivered
milk and eggs, leaving them outside the door on the porch—
and not a metaphor, a way of explaining red hair
and freckles. The clink of glass, the sound of footsteps
in the dark, before the pink hint of a sunrise.

The man drives a truck—there is no horse, though the trick
of memory places one in the story—old, just this side
of the glue factory. The boy lies in bed listening
to the hoofs clomping on a brick pavement.
His window open, the hum of insects before the first crow.

His mother is moving downstairs through the house.
A girl comes to the back door each morning,
the two work the kitchen, skillet and grease.
At school, she would always carry a book with her—
before circumstance—

He waits for the moment his mother will send her
to fetch him for breakfast. He feigns sleep
to draw her closer, feigns sleep just to hear
her voice speak his name. Twice. Then again
before he rolls toward her, reaching.

There is no time, she says.

Seven Seals

We court the end of days as if it were a lover
wearing fine lace—comes into the room
and whispers, you were the one, always.
Carrion eaters—the organist
plays carnival tunes in the cathedral—pilgrims
crawl on hands and knees, seeking
the divine. An old woman knits the names—
her husband who never believed, a drunken uncle,
a sister who preferred dancing,
her children who seem strangers now,
her grandchildren who speak in tongues.

We mutter to each other in ancient Greek—
laughing old stories into our beer.
We meet at Dirty's for the ambiance. You lean
your cheek against *the wall* and cry for young men
you once loved as brothers. You hold
court while I sit knee to knee with
the prettiest girl in the room.

Fireflies and Baseball

The narrative folds like a Sears and Roebuck
catalogue kept in his grandmother's outhouse
next to the chicken coup, ripe with an odor
he associates with feathers.

His grandmother grabs a hen by the neck,
and with a circular jerk, snaps it. Strong fingers.
The hen, part of the pot with dumplings, sweetened tea
in glasses with ice tasting like rust, turnip greens
and Jell-O with canned fruit inside the mold.

In the yard, sitting on metal chairs, they talk
about Carl who served in the first war,
who could bunt a pitched baseball off the end of his bat.
The burning tip of a cigarette punctuating sentences.
They don't play the game that way anymore.

Now batters just swing for the fences.
The men cling to the belief there was a time—
when a handshake and style—take your father's new car
his uncle says, pointing to the '56 Buick—white.
They used to make cars out of steel.

Screws

Toothless if it weren't for modern dentistry—
though we quibble the term,
out of date sixty-five years or more.
A rotary dial, an AM car radio
playing Benny and Godfrey—

Do they remember any of it. Of course not.
Benny lived next door to Crockett, you explain—
both killed at Hastings—Normans speaking French.
Crockett's grandfather—great or great-great,
a star at Louie's court.

The woman at the counter explains insurance
simply won't cover dental implants.
No matter, you tell her, I'm richer than kings.
I have a high definition flat screen at home
and a 9mm Berretta tucked under my shirt.

Saturday

I spend the day shoveling turkey shit and dirt—
plant tomatoes, onions—scatter a few basil
seeds.

Work shirtless, though almost seventy—
too old and wrinkled to work half naked
in the open air—too old to give a shit.
Drink Shiner in the afternoon—
soil and sweat making the beer taste better.

Walter was working his garden when he died—
so we figure—lying in the back yard. The phone ringing
when we arrive—something whispers in my ear,
and I pass quickly through the house to find him
lying on the grass a few yards from the squash—

under a pecan tree.

Something about growing your own food.
It's better than hating immigrants
or worrying over who gets into heaven.

My accountant tells me he probably has less
than five years left—he is seventy-two
with a bad heart. I spend my days listening
to people grumble about paying too much
in taxes, he says. No way to live.

I don't complain, I tell him. He grins.
You believe in taxes, he tells me.

If God—

I lack a faith that will move mountains,
nor believe the meek will inherit—though I am assured
I don't understand the Greek context.

I watch an old high school buddy raise
his hands during worship,
his eyes shut tight in ecstasy.

The same person calls for the annihilation
of the enemy, accepts collateral damage
as part of the baggage—

God will know his own,
says the abbot at Béziers.
Kill them all.

How do I explain—
whatever the ecstasy,
I want no part.

If I am judging—
I take a certain comfort in the color
of the Pacific Ocean, in the taste of black coffee.

Recovering the Body

Some words I look up over
and over—never get them pat.
Etymology and the hermeneutics
of what was meant by that
particular phrase.

I am reading a friend, an acquaintance
really—we should all read him.
Saw him twice or maybe three times
at a writer's festival.

He comes in with this kind of anti-pose
Jude Law, Gigolo Joe have you ever
fucked a poet air that seems to work
for him.

It's bad enough his poems
are really good.

Early March

The sweet smell of bluebonnets reminds me why I love
this place so much, she says. We see the first blossom
this morning—walking the new subdivision.
It grows alone on a patch of dirt and gravel
next to the new road. A roofer nails sheathing
to the deck of a framed house with an air gun in rapid fire—
pop, pop—pop, pop—

holding the trigger and bouncing the gun
along the surface, balancing on the slope—
pop, pop—pop, pop.

A light mist. The banner petals a deep almost
purple blue—white spots. I should love it here
too, he says. A squirrel hops from one branch
to another high in the trees. Buzzards fly
in formation. Before construction began we saw
wild turkeys here.

I Have this House

I have this house
with its newly renovated
upstairs office. I read
and write there—pretend
one can survive

with books and a view
of a field with dried grass,
a pile of sawed off trunks
from dead oaks.

Someone called, wanting them
the other day—the tree trunks.
Take them, I said, but they never
showed.

Interim

Five thousand years of history bent,
the word writ—to keep her spent
and ragged—toothless in metaphor,
if you want the truth of it.

A pin prick or pen—
ink smeared on her cheek,
the spin of gold, the name withheld, untold—
We will crush the earth,
if we must.

She fusses with her hair—deliberately
causing the train to be late.

He waits at the station with a letter
in his coat pocket—folded and unfolded
a dozen times. There is no God,
she tells him, only the hope
of sex during the game.

Meeting Only Once

Bits of sand sting his face,
his chin tucked against his jacket as he walks
the gap between buildings—

the wind flapping his pants.

Earlier that morning a girl comes into the dorm,
arms folded around her books.
He stands in the hall with a towel

wrapped around his waist—how thin
he was then—and while she sees him,
she turns the corner and climbs the stairs—

several steps before she stops.
I'm in the wrong building, she says,
more to herself than to him.

It all depends, he tells her and smiles.
She turns and descends the stairs,
clutching her books tightly.

Memorial Day–1980

The body of a young man hangs
in a tree the next morning—
cars stacked three deep at the Toyota dealership,
the gym floor at the old rec center
swollen, buckling.

Pick up games played
on Saturday mornings—or at noon
during the week when men would skip
lunch for forty minutes
of make it-take it, elbows and hips—grunts.

A piano from the music store,
baptized in the swollen current,
left in the street.

At night, a boat rescues a woman
from the roof of her house—the camera
records the scene, her eyes wide with wonder,
lights in her face.

This is amazing, she says.
Did you lose anything, the reporter asks.
Oh yes, everything, she says, still smiling.
Simply everything.

Glass

The end of the world occurs
in October—classmates talk about quitting
school, joining the army,
like our fathers—
raised on the notion that every generation—

My mother graduated in '43. The boys
had already left by then. Marries on a whim
one afternoon when the sun is shining
on someone she barely knows.

Young men in uniform crowd
train stations. The best of days,
my mother says.

In October, trees are reduced to char,
an eagle scorched in flight, a daisy falls from
the hand of a small child. The sky blackens.
A coke bottle tied to the string of a venetian blind—

The first time a girl kisses me—her lips on mine,
how water should taste, how the grass grows,
the smell of honey suckles.

My grandmother sings
as she works the kitchen, preparing breakfast.
The smell of bacon in a skillet.

Tucked Away in a Drawer

Once, at baseball tryouts in Huntsville—the old prison
looming, whispering—my father, having sipped
deeply from a pint of bourbon, schooled us
on the smell of sex as if all regrets began
and ended in the nose. It's hard to explain,
he mumbled, how one can yearn for it—

The subject even now remains taboo—one can't
speak openly—but tells so much about a man
who wrote desperate letters from Italy
during the war to his young wife—fearful letters
to a girl he barely knew, but not letters
fearful of the war.

Stay sweet, was the recurring plea. Stay sweet,
he wrote to a woman he couldn't believe married him.

I read the letters, the handwriting a crowded mix
of cursive and print and discover myself standing
in Delmore's darkened theater, the son who cries out
from a distant future. I am ushered up the aisle.
It's not too late, I tell them—but it was.

One does not cry out in a theater—
nor talk openly about the smell of sex.

How different we were from each other,
my father and me.

A Person of Interest

Danny and I change out the water pump
and thermostat on my daughter's car.
The day before we had driven my pickup
pulling an open trailer from Austin to El Paso,
stopping in Ft. Stockton for hamburgers.
My daughter and her friend were coming
home after a year of work and school.

That morning we had packed the trailer
and were ready to leave when she told
us her car had been overheating.
I had almost forgotten that she had lived
in the same city where I attended sixth grade.
Almost forgotten the water pump and the night

long drive back home. That night
someone placed a bomb in the Olympic park
in Atlanta, the bomber expressing his opposition
to abortion. I had almost forgotten that the guard
who saved many lives was falsely implicated,
that the bomber struck again and again.
We pulled into Austin at daylight.

Desperado

Where I live there are no bars, Berryman says,
or where he vaguely lives—I am thinking iron
on a door or window and not where one can sit
with Rumi or Hank. Where I live vaguely, he mutters
into his coffee cold. I feel old—

He tries to avoid the camera's eye—everywhere mounted.
One can't scratch an itch without being documented
and posted for his in-laws, former students, ex lovers,
potential assassins—filed and counted among the lost.
Scrapes his toast with butter and jam.

Here I am, he says to no one in particular,
sitting between summer and summer, toenails
having grown thick, eyebrows bushy—
he says to a yellow pencil on his desk,
remembering an old dialogue he once recited.

Empty Gestures

A man I don't know squares off with me
in the aisle of a grocery store. Why don't you just
shut up, he says, glaring. I am off guard,
but line the cart between the man and me
in case. Yes, you—he hisses.

His eyes burn. I don't know you,
I want to say, but instead grip the handle
tightly, my confusion shifting to a kind of anger.
A store manager, intercedes. Escorts the guy
out of the store. I am alone with my wife.

I really wanted to ram him, I mutter. Let it go,
she tells me. But I find myself hoping
the son of a bitch is waiting for me outside.
I look for him. What did you say, the manager asks
me when he returns to the store.

While Yet My Tongue

You gotta goes along to get along, the speaker says.
Looks round the room. There's people missing here.
They didn't go along—he dances a soft shoe
on a sprinkled saw dust floor. Tells a joke or two—
every laughs—except our poet in the corner.

Weep! Weep! Weep! he mumbles—the page turner,
heretic, freethinker, tinker, pinker—in soot
he sleeps. Where are you Blake when we need—
when one teaches the verse as witness to grace,
poor Tom freed by death.

Just be a good boy, and God will be your father.
Just serve the master like a good boy,
and God—It's the lion that makes them rules,
the speaker says. It's true, the preacher confirms.
And the dean—of marketing who once claimed

Eichmann ethical because he simply followed
the law. The law being the law. He mutters to himself,
and wonders how much longer God—looks to the rafters
in an empty church at night. How much longer—

Blood Ties

No matter how I work
the floor—evenings after the store
closes—mop and bucket
suds splashed liberally on tile,
erasing foot traffic—

Penelope figures the daily tape.
You show up late, crusty—smelling
of ale and blood,
wanting to confront someone or something—
old demons, your own dim reflection
in the store front glass,
something in me.

The narrative of diminishing stars,
a drop of rain—

We take inventory and order pizza.
I slip a bottle of I.W. Harper out the back
door when tossing empty boxes.

Sabbath

The stomach growls—we were hungry—
never mind Pharisee hand wringing.
Saturday was supposed to be a day off—
softball, hot dogs, a cold beer.

He once hit a ball so square,
it sailed over the tall pines
behind center field,
the moment perfectly attuned.

That evening, we drive to Bethesda,
timing contractions—a first child—
walk the parking lot for hours.

In Tennessee a guy looking like Christ,
stands on the side of the road and holds
out his thumb, but there was no room
in the car.

When the Preacher Absent Mindedly

Slumped over in an agave mood, clanking
keys on an old manual—you can't find them anymore—
the Underwood sitting on his desk, the radio playing
—his teacher comes into the room and weeps
openly—a perceptive shift. Clanking words
with fingers numb, he sips the sting slowly.

An old lover warns the world is held loosely
together by an old Russian foe—anyone better
than the post colonial, regardless of birth—Kenyan.
Arrogantly speaking, so to speak—the man talks
in complete sentences for God's sake.
What to make of it all.

Grace before a fall—He stands in the street,
listens to the sky cracking open. A shadow whispers
in his ear—Have you accepted… When I was a boy,
he answers. Accepted it all, dunked in the cold smell
of chlorine. On the preacher's wrist, a watch—

Which O Witch

I am a prodigal come home, but not to a waiting
father's embrace—nor did he give me my inheritance
when I left, nor did I ask for it. Still, he claimed—
spoke of my ingratitude. The boy was always
difficult, he would tell friends.

I was scolded by them more than once for failing—
yes, I would say, admitting to crimes not committed,
but crimes nevertheless—being born was enough.

When I am ten, my brother and I, along with the twins,
climb Mount Scott near Ft. Sill, Oklahoma. Jader
drops us off at the bottom of the climb and drives
on to the top. He will meet us half way, he says.
July, and we work our way up the rocks.

My brother gets stuck on a ridge. I am up ahead,
higher, too afraid to shimmy down the smooth stone face
to help him. Later we drink cokes, while Jader
swigs his beer, crushes the hard metal cans with one hand.
I expect you to be able when we meet next—

But we never—

I listen to a woman read about being an army brat.
I wonder for a moment if she might be—connected
somehow, a daughter perhaps of one of the twins—
a look familiar, but only a wish.

The cokes were ice cold. When I was eight,
I kissed one of the twins on the cheek outside
the service club during play practice—on a small
army base on the edge of Cayey.

At my father's funeral, I sing a note softly
in my sister's ear. *Ding.* She looks at me
wide eyed, and in disbelief sings softly back.
Dong.

Chopper

If we could but hang together—the plea, the cry
of a soul desperate for some inkling of light—once
rode in Hueys, you want to tell someone,
but the bellies of your children are growling,
heaven knows why you suffered them into the world,
wide eyed and snot nosed, looking nothing
like you expected.

One cries herself to sleep, the other more stoic,
sits upright in bed counting to herself
—three, four, lock the door.

You once killed a man, you want to explain—
in another place where time was measured
by moonless nights, when no matter how hard
you tried to stay awake—a dream perhaps.

You wait in line. The guy in front of you turns
and ask if you've ever been in reform school.
Have you ever—the barbed wire strands atop the fence
leaning in—you should have known. It's so dark,
you can't see shit or your fingers.

You grab a job washing dishes at a Denny's.

You hope for a deliverance of some kind—
a guy in a white pickup truck with a six pack
of beer and a plan to sell watermelons
on the side of the road—We go down to Mexico,
to pick up the melons, he says, and you listen.

You once killed a man, you want to tell him.

Wrath

Ezra is old and crazy—locked away for weeks
after the second war in an outdoor cage—muttering,
muttering—Actaeon, Actaeon—hunter
turned stag for gazing on beauty too earnestly.
The dogs tear at his flesh. Ezra loyal
to his friends, and they to him—or some
were. As good as a poet can expect.

Handsome, one might say when young,
weren't we all, but even old and crazy—
a glimmering fire seems to burn.
No one assigned him when I was in school—
Of my friends, only Mark, but then I have
an increasingly smaller circle who bother
with the matter.

All the great poems have been written,
an old navy buddy once wrote me. But have you
read them. Can you name—
He cries to his comrades, and the hunter
becomes the hunted. I am here, he cries.
I am here. I am here.

The Birds Chirp

My brother and I talk about dying—he walks
a cancer time line, I am treading blind.
Toward the end, I want you to make me take
these morning walks, he says—not to bring
up an unpleasant subject. I've never been
able to make you do anything, I say.

Just encourage me, he replies. We listen
to the birds. One chirps, look at the two
old men walking the road. Nothing to worry
about, another responds—no guns.
As boys we were a menace, carrying air
rifles and shooting at anything that moved,

once hitting a sparrow in flight, a blind luck
shot. The sparrow falls lifeless to the ground.
We stare at each other half in amazement,
half in a kind of horror. But boys don't learn
quickly—only vaguely aware that the world
might be real, the sparrow actually dead.

I once killed a deer, I say. We watch a doe
and two fawns scamper across the road.
I shot it more to prove, I think, more to know
if I could when needed—growing up in the Army—
raised on war and rumors.

Writing in the Dust

You can't beat common sense
into the head of a stupid man, she says,
no matter how big the hammer—
and the room agrees, or at least nods
while muttering some variation of *Om*
or *Hmmm* as if confronted with some
incontrovertible truth.

Though if common sense were—
it wouldn't be so rare, the poet suggests.
Who among us, he continues as if to offer
a first stone, a smooth flat rock
picked up next to the river, better
suited for skipping, slung in submarine
motion low across the water—

is without a moment or two. Who
among us could carry the burden—
he says. But there is always some idiot
willing to try.

In Session

The world binges on lunacy,
he mutters—lip syncing someone else's
voice actually—tones a third step lower
than his own. Some ghost, some longed
for dead friend, he imagines.

Not his father. No, not him—
though the old man haunts his dreams.
Comes back fleshy from the grave,
demands his share of the business,
showers in the master bath.

Our character wakes in a cold sweat. Grumbles
in a voice, not his, about the world crumbling,
too much to drink, too much to think—
about. Tyrants and bullies crowd the tables
at Scholz Garten—you once worked there—

small delicate hands—chintzy tippers.

She Looks at Him Deeply

If a lie it were—told sweetly
with earnest eyes.
How do I love—with quarters
in my pocket, wearing loafers
without socks.

We'd be so much happier
if you stuck your shirttail in,
hand on my shoulder,
words whispered as if dictates
from Sinai.

A letter in the box: *Greetings*—
they don't send them anymore—
from the President—a personal note.
You have been selected—
summoned by—after watching you bathe
one summer night on the roof.

An honor, cummings's father would have said
if only he could speak—
having been laid out dead in the sod.
You nod weak and unbuckle your belt.
Not here, you idiot—though merely
and thoughtlessly complying.

Free Breakfast

I am the first in the breakfast room at a motel
in Van Horn—pour a cup of batter on the waffle iron
and flip it, a cup of coffee, scrambled eggs and sausage—
thinking of my heart. Talking heads on the flat screen.
A middle aged woman comes in and looks at the pitcher
of milk, tells the young man working the desk to pour
it out, clean the pitcher, and refill it with fresh milk.

I am supposed to be on vacation, but nothing gets done
right when I'm not here, she tells me. These young people—
The slender young man takes the pitcher to the back somewhere.
These young people, the woman says again.
A green light, and I pick the golden waffle from the iron
with a plastic fork. I am not that hungry,
but the food is part of the fare—free breakfast.

Steve once told me he considered moving to this place
in the Texas high desert to work on the novel.
Nothing else to do, he said.

A Footrace

He makes a resistor using a #2 pencil and some copper
wiring he strips from an extension chord because it is Sunday,
and the stores are closed. An old black and white
Philco is restored—for now. A couple of weeks,
he tells us with prophetic accuracy. It's football season,
so a couple of weeks count.

He taught himself to repair television sets
in the 1950s, using manuals and an old TV he picked
up as junk. A little cash on the side—the town electrical
genius, though he never finished high school.
The company eventually promoted him from driving
a truck to the lab.

He challenged us once, my brother and me, to a foot
race up a hill. He was mid thirties, I was eighteen
and underestimated—a story he chuckled about
for years. When his daughter was killed, he raised
her two youngest children without complaint.
One evening when the air was thick with honeysuckles,

he talked about missing her, but he was always
more comfortable explaining diodes.

Passing the Torch

Some ancient dream—if only God would destroy
his enemies, and maybe half his friends
for good measure. David, on his dying bed,
hands Solomon a list of men he promised
not to kill, whispers in his best Marlon
Brando impersonation, his jowls puffed.
Solomon dutifully adds his brother's name.

He watches the candidate boast, the children
will be taught to honor and respect,
children every one will recite—in unison
their undying pledge. A bronze statue should be erected,
he says—of me. In the middle of the city.

There will be no place left to run, no place to hide—
the bashing of skulls against the rocks.
A knock on the door at night—men enter
the house and take the poets and would be poets
with them to some deserted road—headlights
of cars, engines running.

One Small Step

My grandmother arrived from Alabama
in a wagon and left in a Cadillac.
Wore a bonnet while picking cotton
to shade the sun. Hand pumped water
from a shallow well under her back porch.
Lost a son in the second world war.

She witnessed Neil stepping on the moon's
surface leaving imprints in the dust.

A car turns and heads for Dike Bridge,
Ophelia drowns, and Hamlet swims
back to the hotel where in his room,
he removes his wet clothes, collapses
on his bed, the window open—

Not Yet

You are slipping awkwardly into the space
between—shoulder and toes tingling
from some kind of nerve damage, you suppose—
your ears and nose—the notion of growing old
gracefully giving way to bumping into a coffee table
while navigating a dark room—you knew
the table was there—a sharp pain, the thump
of wood to bone, the shin screams.

You moan. You fall. You lie on the floor
thinking you should get up—
or maybe you could just close your eyes
and stay there. Yes—

Not yet, something whispers in your ear.

Hunter

Skin pitted black from work and soot,
hands calloused, forearms knotted—
dank sweat, cold drenching
sweat, salt stained flannel shirt—
a thermos of black coffee, a tin pail
carried in the dark that morning.

The tobacco smell of men. She sings
as she moves through the kitchen. Biscuits
rise, grease fried eggs—the house
holding memory, feather mattress
imprints. Stories of wolves and faithful
dogs and bears. A single shot twelve

gauge hangs above the door jam—
loaded. He carries it into the field.
He is ten or eleven. He listens
to the chirping of birds. The feel
of the stock against his cheek.
It is December—the world asleep.

Forbidden

In a crowded elevator, your hand
touches my hip and lingers long enough
for me to take note, then you drop it to your side.
A sweet indiscretion, a moment never really
repeated, the narrative lost in circumstance,
the confusion of memory and desire—

It's raining again today—after years of drought,
. it rains and rains. The lake is swollen—beautiful
though threatening. Thunder rumbles. We live
on high ground—lightening strikes are common.
But we will not drown here.

Still, I feel I am under water—deep.

We meet at a coffee shop and talk about poetry
and lovers, about sitting in a parking lot
when a cop taps on the car window and asks
for IDs. What are you doing here, in official tones.
Just talking. Is that okay with you, you snap back.

I'm impressed with the audacity of your response.
Is that okay with you—not asking permission,
not even close. We sip our coffee, and you confess
you don't remember the incident. You, on the other hand
remember everything, you say slightly annoyed.

That was just something that happened
a long time ago. I sip my coffee, looking at my cup—
my hands. Fragile clay, I mutter to the table.
What—nothing. The coffee shop now distant,
and it is raining.

Sawdust

We once rode the Ferris wheel, you and I,
at the state fairgrounds—was it October or later
in the year, I can't remember. We marched
in a parade there—later, you and I paired up
and rode the Ferris wheel together.

By the time it reached the top, I was easily in love
with you. I watched you looking at the people
below. You were smiling, lips together—
sitting next to me. A moment kept in a drawer
with a post card autographed by Stan Musial,
Ken Boyer—Minnie Minsoso that one season
he played for the Cardinals.

I gave the card away a few years ago to a guy
who seemed delighted to have it. But I kept
the ride. The grounds covered with sawdust.

Uncle Wants You

The machine gun in the Great War rendered the epic warrior
irrelevant, he explains. The epic poet with him,
though Ezra complains and keeps writing. Read him with a thick
companion if you must, his beard rust or dust—treason
being relative to who not what.

We hunker in the mud, dreaming—et cetera. Cummings
a poor substitute for socks, not to mention—
flea proof love. Mud covers everything, cakes the skin,
the eyebrows—he watches her walk across campus
on a November afternoon, the wind blows her hair back,
the grit stings her face.

Did she even know. His companion suggests they go
to the gym, then a night of poker. This was before
the cops dragged him down from a pole in an all night
café, before he squatted on a hillside—a moonless night
when he couldn't even see his fingers.

Keeping the Files

My family prides itself on its memory—sharp
and vivid—though no two of us remember a single
event the same. Point of view, my aunt says.
My sister simply claims we coexists in parallel
dimensions, touching but distinctive.

Not exactly the way I explained it, my sister
tells me. Who really won the footrace up the hill
to the old school is lost in the telling, as well
as who actually ran it. Never mind, who kissed
my mother while she and a boy squatted behind

the high curb of the old gravel street, the men
at the store spying them. That wasn't your mother,
a middle sister says. That was me. And we all agree
she is wrong, even though half of us weren't born
to witness. Still we remember.

3 AM

I bury my head in the covers,
the morning hours away. The cold
room. I listen for rat scratches, an old habit.
We set out poison when nothing else worked.
A leather carcass found under the dishwasher
when replaced last month.

I listen—no scratching. Still the house hums
like an old gypsy calling the dead.
Do you believe in the soul, or is everything weighed
with a scale made of silver, polished once a week
on Friday. Do you remember when we showered
in water so hot it turned our skin a bright red.

I lay in bed waiting for sleep to catch me—
dreamed I was running.

Before Drinking a Cold Beer

I work in the heat—sweat saturates my shirt,
my shorts, stings my eyes a little. A small cloud
gives a moment of relief. It's too hot, you say.
Yes, but it's always hot here in summer.

It rained all winter and spring. The lakes swelled
to the brim—wildflowers colored the fields—
but now the drought is slated to return—la Niña—
when the ground cracks like an old woman's skin.

That we are part of the equation—more than just
a butterfly flapping its wings in the Amazon—
seems certain, though greed—Grimms' stepmother
of necessity—disagrees.

I work in the heat as a form of penance, I think—
something to appease whatever. I chant to myself
as I work. No pain, no fear, no desire—a mantra
of sorts. I feel the sun on my neck.

Digression

A point-misser,
a bitter-ender,
a carnival barker,
a trickster, loser, blueser—
played in twelve bar progressions
on an empty stage.

It's the age we live in.
Filming decapitations
with smart phones—
Take possession and own it,
his analyst says peering from her notes
as if one could grab hold

and stop the rotation of the Earth.
A two year old child flops down
on a tiled floor and kicks at the air—
I sure as shit didn't choose this,
he screams. The woman pours
cream in her coffee. The man drinks
his black.

Empirical

Sarah tells us the Earth will still be beautiful
after we're gone—gone meaning all—salamanders,
butterflies, trees, whales, fleas—all.
Since my earliest prayers—*if I die before*
I wake, I pray the Lord my soul—
have known since the fifth grade when we were told—
the extinction of the sun.

Almost everything we think we know,
the speaker says, almost everything we believe—
how easily we deceive. *If we are to keep*
the lights on, we will simply have to kill—
people a few shades browner than we are—
speaking as if from a distance.

And Now...

Coming to fruition during or lagging
behind the war—ovens still warm,
imagines 1941 never happened, to pick
the year arbitrarily as if from a deck
of cards—the ace of spades.

I call it as I see it, he says. Back seat
love on a gravel road—before the dam,
before the lake, the Kingsmen singing
the only song we ever really needed.
What were the fucking words—

There's the rub. The ones one can say
openly in church, like burning crispy
in a lake of fire, but never kissing
with your lips open—the mystery
of being French, living in Paris
in 1890, attending the ballet.

Walking the curb on a bridge
at night, the snow falling on a bleak
land, a lonely land. I've read tomes,
he cries out, been drunk in the homes
of the great and the fallen.

In love once or twice, he admits.

Moonlighting

We skinny dip with another couple
one night in the Gulf—Galveston.
The ghost of Jean Lafitte dancing
with us in the surf, the waves crashing.
Skipping naked and free.

The way artists and writers live,
we tell ourselves, wanting it to be true.
I type stories on a portable Olympia—
stories about a young man failing

to make the grade at a St. Louis Cardinal
try out camp in Texas, grounding out
to second base in an only time at bat.
Driving home later trying to digest

what he should have known all along.
I think something bit me, the guy
with us says. He had been teaching
at Princeton, but failed to get tenure.

It was then we notice the crabs.

Morning Constitutional

A cotton shirt clinging to skin—moist even
this early when the sun barely clears the trees
lining the edge of the old field where Ford
and Dobbin once grazed cattle—each to each,
but held on common ground. One man worked
with wood the other concrete. Both yearned
more for the days when ranching proved
adequate, if those days were indeed…

I worked with Ford one summer building
barracks on base. He helped construct the forms
for concrete pillars, I pushed mud
in a wheel barrow and moved bricks using
tongs—shoulders and arms aching some,
sweat salting the back of my shirt—
one summer when drinking two cream sodas
for lunch was the best part of the day.

Years later, Dobbin would pour foundations
for our houses. Ford died three decades back.
Today, we walk the road past the old field
where cows sought shelter in the shade
of live oaks. A copperhead suns itself
on the pavement. It turns to strike as we pass.

Horseflies

I take his temperature using an ear
thermometer. He is running a fever. A few days
earlier they placed a tube in his jugular, and now
if he moves the wrong way, it hurts. He messages
the nurse to call him.

I find myself weighing things, he tells us, but I tend
to go along.

A horsefly stings my back—walking the river—
swatting with my cap. They never bother me
when I'm walking with you, he says—sweet blood.
The nurse calls, and tells him to come in.
I'll drive myself, my brother says when my wife offers.

Earning Our Keep

Rain lilies sprout in my yard after four days of downpour—
Six-pointed white earth stars on a blessed day,
Angela writes. Short lived blossoms on spindly stems.
I count them as if they were candles on a cake,
but lose myself in the numbers—losing ground
in the game of what might have been.

Still, beauty in a single blossom holds the world
in place. A list of things to do, the utility of getting through.
A registration sticker to be placed on the windshield—
I play the game of doing one useful thing a day,
that would be enough. We walk with the birds
in the morning.

My wife takes the boy to the doctor to have his cast
removed.

Floss

My uncle lies in a hospital bed,
days from dying—pancreatic
cancer—does anyone have dental floss,
he asks. My aunt rummages her purse,
but comes up empty. Does anyone, my
uncle pleads—I have some in my pocket.

Thank you, he says—works the thread
between his perfect teeth, gap at a time.
When he died a week later, in his last moments,
he climbed unsteadily from his bed,
made his way to the nurse's station,
and hugged each and every goodbye.
It did not please my aunt.

Scott says we can pretend there's no such thing
as metaphor, we can pretend. Dental floss
is just dental floss. But perfect teeth
demand a certain appreciation. A man
just fifty-one and dying still clings,
even after one is resigned—

Literary Ghosts

Not where one expects good news—
only perhaps not as bad as one feared.
People slump in their chairs, alone
or in pairs, bubbled off, each in private
meditation.

My brother says he needs to leave
his phone with me when they take him
back for the procedure—someone may call
about a rain barrel—but we forget.

I take the elevator to the lobby to buy
coffee—we may have a cup left, the woman
says shaking the thermos. I buy water
instead and return to the waiting room.

A veteran, younger than I am, sits next to me,
tells me they just put a six inch needle
in his spine. You ever been shot, he asks.
This feels worse than being shot.

A nurse brings him a wheelchair.
Are you still feeling some discomfort,
she asks. I look for my copy of *National
Geographic.* Feel myself sliding off the edge—

of the earth. It seems I've spent half
my life in hospital waiting rooms, I mutter
to Marley who sits opposite me, chained
to his chair. Old Marley, how we should

have danced more. The old ghost grins
as if the grin were code to some buried secret.

A Focal Point

My sister at two is found standing naked
on the back porch with an unlit cigarette
dangling from her lips. She shits in my shoe—
she says because I wouldn't pay her any mind.
Probably true, my memories of her more cloud
than rain. But how would she remember.

My second daughter claims to remember events
before she was born, so who is to know.
I feel a twitch of pain, an evening at Ford's
Theater—the world turns. Do we share
memory with atoms in the air—

At four my sister decides to run away.
She packs a bag and heads out the door,
down the street. We wave goodbye,
and she collapses on the pavement and cries—

Each to Each

The center of the world is here—he pins the spot
in a straw grass field—declares it for queen
and country, will gladly shed what is required,
blood if asked, sweat and grind—the air smelling
of saw dust. He grips the handle of a tool—
shovel, hoe, sword, spear—the real of it is lost
in the glaze.

I find you in an empty room— you look up
from your book, not all that pleased to see me.

He drives to a desert mountain town to drink tequila
with an old war buddy. They sink into the pine wood
floor while the bartender pours another shot. Shares
an old tale without speaking. He leaves and makes
his way down an alley in the darkness, his feet dancing
on the edge of the solar system.

Finds the old house, abandoned now—a shattered
window. Shimmies the door lock and enters—
the rooms bare. Moonlight.

You look up from your book.

Song to a Dying Tree

There is no English word for a parent
who has lost a child nor a sister or brother
who has lost a sibling—or none that I know.
No orphan or widow, simply one left behind,
as if the rapture—does it call up or swallow.

We seek each other out sometimes, standing
in pairs like wounded soldiers or birds
whose wings—

When the worst has happened, you tell yourself
this is the worst that can happen—a talisman of sorts.
But you know better.

A spider's web clings between
the twigs of a live oak, the tree itself slowly
dying from drought and oak wilt. You press
your cheek against its bark and whisper
in a tone only it will understand.

Carbon

It's easy to assume if you never really grieved
before, then perhaps you never really loved before.
It's easy to assume such things. A fish swimming
in a cold river. If so, you can only be thankful
in a way not easy to explain.

You've read what they say. None of it's true,
though we all nod and pretend to agree.
The river is still cold, but deeper—no getting
to the bottom of it. There is the mind of God,
the will of God, to wrestle with, if you choose.

The pain of a dislocated hip might offer
some relief—face to face. What is your name—
one who comes behind, heel grabber—
a favorite son sold into bondage—goat's blood
splattered on a coat.

You mourn for four thousand years—until you drop
acid on a farm in New York—lose your memory
in the mud and rain. Dance half naked in the mud
and rain with a girl calling herself Rachel. Dance half naked
in the mud and rain—what is your name—

He Addresses a Class Early in the Semester

He watches baseball in the evening and pretends
the world exists between the lines—who's on first,
if one bothers with the matter at all—yes.
No longer America's game, but he settles
into the play by play with memories of a boy
who swings at pitches imagined, watches
the spin of the ball—a 34 inch wooden bat,
hands calloused—a hundred times or more
in the back yard at night with fireflies.

San Francisco Giant tryout camp in Huntsville,
the pitch low and inside—a called third strike
when anyone with eyes—
He walks to the dugout—knowing
even then it would be as close as he would
ever get—the smell of summer grass.

Only one thing kept me from the show,
he tells his class years later—pauses
for effect. Just one little thing, his finger
and thumb held half an inch apart.
Nothing really lost, when he thinks it through,
as if he had shed a heavy cloak
and walked away free—though it took awhile.
What—the students look at him.

Talent, he smiles.

Punctuation

I've discovered a new favorite tequila—
one shouldn't perhaps celebrate finding
a new favorite brand, considering genetic
tendencies toward a brooding darkness,
an oppressive heaviness of a man leaning
into a boy, headlock suffocating—the boy comes
out of it swinging—but it sips well and slow.

Here in the bar, we enjoy a moment after
working dirt in the afternoon, sun sweating
through our shirts and shorts, swigging water
by the quart, after pizza and beer—here
where the bartender works smoothly
making cocktails, then he pours a straight shot
of a reposado that bites just enough.

I pose with my hand wrapping the glass
like an old gunslinger. But there is no holstered
pistol, open or concealed. It's just an attitude
taken from all the movies we watched
as kids, growing up in Texas—or California.
It's a good day, the gunslinger says to his youngest
daughter. Yes, she says. It is.

Notes, references, and allusions to other works—

"A Bakery Revisited"—The first stanzas are reacting to Elizabeth Bishop's "Going to the Bakery." Virginia in the poem is the state of Virginia.

"Dots on the Horizon"—How he imagines the incoming fighters first appeared on June 8, 1967.

"Beginning Its Fall"—Begins with reference to a scene in Thomas Pynchon's *Gravity's Rainbow.*

"Gathering"—Begins with a reference to Ezra Pounds.

"Sleeps Through the Morning Alarm"—The man and woman meeting on a street corner is from a scene imagined, viewed from another upstairs window in Virginia Woolf's *A Room of One's Own.*

"Measuring Gaps"—Bozeman, Montana, the red-winged blackbird, and the boy refer to a place and a scene in Robert Pirsig's *Zen and the Art of Motorcycle Maintenance.* The manual is John Muir's *How to Keep Your Volkswagen Alive.*

"I Shall Pick the Flowers Myself"—The title alludes to *Mrs. Dalloway.* "...before the light of shell fire revealed the world—puffed and stuffed with straw" alludes to *A Room of One's Own* and "The Hollow Men."

"If You Feel Like Clapping Your Hands"—Gil is Gil Scott-Heron.

"Love Letter #2471"—Lorca in the produce section appears in Alan Ginsberg's "A Supermarket in California."

"Trick or Treat"—Some echoes from Mary Robison's "Yours" can be found here.

"Shine"—Richard Brautigan was the first writer I remember using the term "Volstead Act days" in "Revenge of the Lawn."

"Seven Seals"—The old woman in the poem is an echo of the terrible grandmother in Sandra Cisneros "Mericans." The wall is the Vietnam memorial in DC. Dirty's is a hamburger joint in Austin.

"Interim"—References to Sleeping Beauty and Rumpelstiltskin then echoes from the opening scene in *Franny and Zooey*.

"Tucked Away in A Drawer"—Delmore's darkened theater alludes to Delmore Schwartz's "In Dreams Begin Responsibilities."

"Desperado"—The no bars refers to John Berryman's *Dream Songs* 200. Rumi is Rumi. Hank is Charles Bukowski.

"While Yet My Tongue"—Poor Tom alludes to William Blake's "The Chimney Sweeper: When my mother died I was very young." The rafters in an empty church alludes to the movie "Cool Hand Luke." I did work in a school where a dean claimed that Adolf Eichmann acted ethically because he was following the law.

"Which O Witch"—Allusions to the "Wizard of Oz."

"Wrath"—*Alludes to Ezra Pound's "Fourth Canto."*

"She Looks at Him Deeply"—cummings's narrator's father appears in "my sweet old etcetera."

"Uncle Wants You"—Ezra is Ezra Pounds. *The second stanza alludes to ee cummings "my sweet etcetera."*

"Digression"—Kristen in Steve Erickson's *The Sea Came in at Midnight* uses the term point-misser. I've not seen it anywhere else. John Berryman gives us a bitter-ender in *Dream Songs 182.*

"Empirical"—Refers to a Sarah Webb poem I read on Facebook.

"And Now…"—Imagines 1941 never happened and living in Paris in 1980 come from Anne Sexton's "Walking in Paris."

"Literary Ghosts"—The copy of National Geographic alludes to Elizabeth Bishop's "In the Waiting Room." The ghost of Jacob Marley makes an appearance in this poem.

"Carbon"—Echoes of Jacob wrestling with the angel, or the Lord, or with Esau from *Genesis.*

Author Bio—I first came across Geronimo's reported last words used in my bio in the short documentary *Grave Misgivings* by Jeffrey Palmer and Constance Squires. I also found them in a PBS *American Experience* series, *We Shall Remain: Geronimo.*

Brady Peterson was born in Ft. Sill, Oklahoma in the shadow of the second world war, also perhaps in the shadow of Geronimo who when he died reportedly confessed to his nephew, "I should have never surrendered. I should have fought until I was the last man alive." As kids we would yell his name when we jumped from tree limbs, the poet says. Brady is the author of *Glued to the Earth, Between Stations,* and *Dust.*